Here is our neighborhood.

Come see some people
and places in it.

Here is our school.

Here is a teacher.

Here is a crossing guard.

Here is our library.

Here is a mail worker.

Here is a trash worker.

Here is a firefighter.

Here is our fire station.

Here is a police officer.

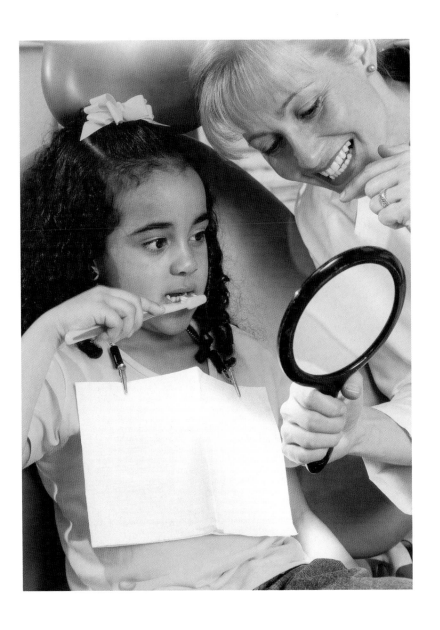

Here is a dentist.

Here is a nurse.

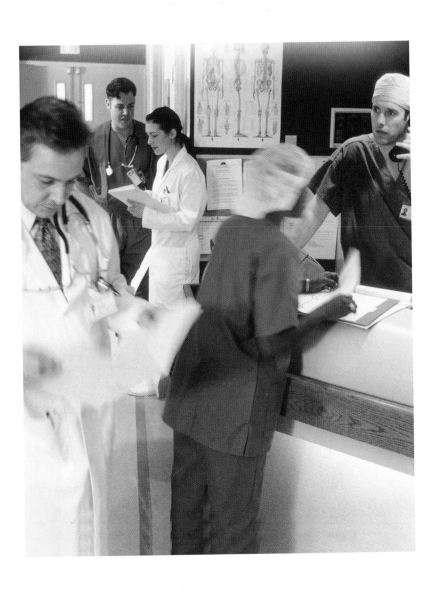

Here is our hospital.

Here is our grocery store.

Here is a cook.

Here is our park.

Do you like our
neighborhood?